Animal Groups

Mollusks

By Dalton Rains

www.littlebluehousebooks.com

Copyright © 2024 by Little Blue House, Mendota Heights, MN 55120. All rights reserved. No part of this book may be reproduced or utilized in any form or by any means without written permission from the publisher.

Little Blue House is distributed by North Star Editions:
sales@northstareditions.com | 888-417-0195

Produced for Little Blue House by Red Line Editorial.

Photographs ©: Shutterstock Images, cover, 4, 7 (top), 7 (bottom), 9, 11 (top), 11 (bottom), 13, 15 (top), 15 (bottom), 17, 19, 21, 22–23, 24 (top left), 24 (top right), 24 (bottom left), 24 (bottom right)

Library of Congress Control Number: 2023902031

ISBN
978-1-64619-811-5 (hardcover)
978-1-64619-840-5 (paperback)
978-1-64619-897-9 (ebook pdf)
978-1-64619-869-6 (hosted ebook)

Printed in the United States of America
Mankato, MN
082023

About the Author

Dalton Rains writes and edits nonfiction children's books. He lives in Minnesota.

Table of Contents

Mollusks **5**

Is It a Mollusk? **22**

Glossary **24**

Index **24**

Mollusks

Some animals are mollusks.

All mollusks have soft bodies.

Many have hard shells.

Slugs are mollusks.

Some live in water.

Others live on land.

7

Clams are mollusks.
Their shells have
two parts.

Oysters and mussels are mollusks.

They live in water.

Scallops are mollusks. Their shells can have bright colors.

Octopuses and squids are mollusks.

They have no shell.

They have many arms.

Cuttlefish are mollusks.

They have spots
and stripes.

They can change colors.

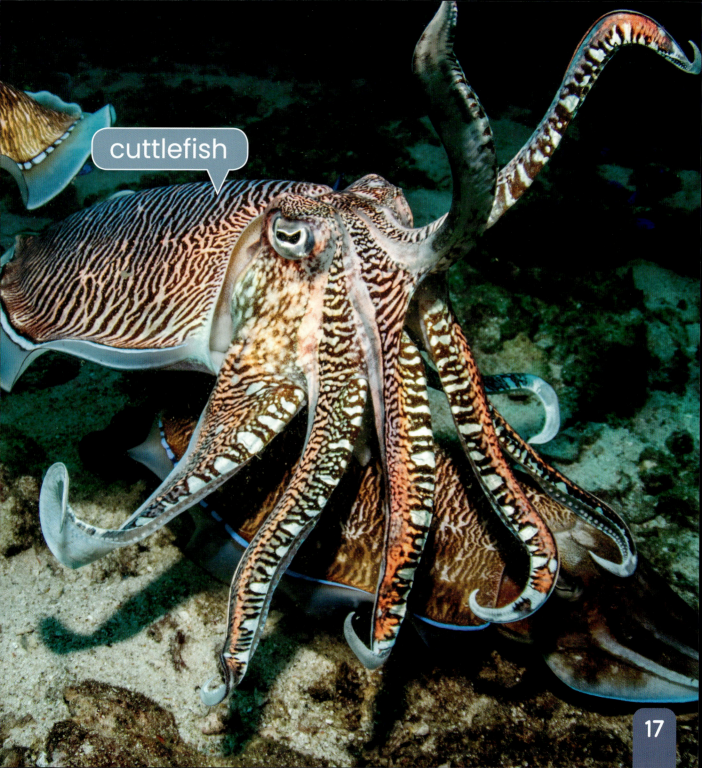

Many mollusks have a type of foot.
The snail uses its foot to climb leaves.

A clam can stretch its foot out of its shell.

Then it can dig.

Is It a Mollusk?

Most mollusks have hard shells.

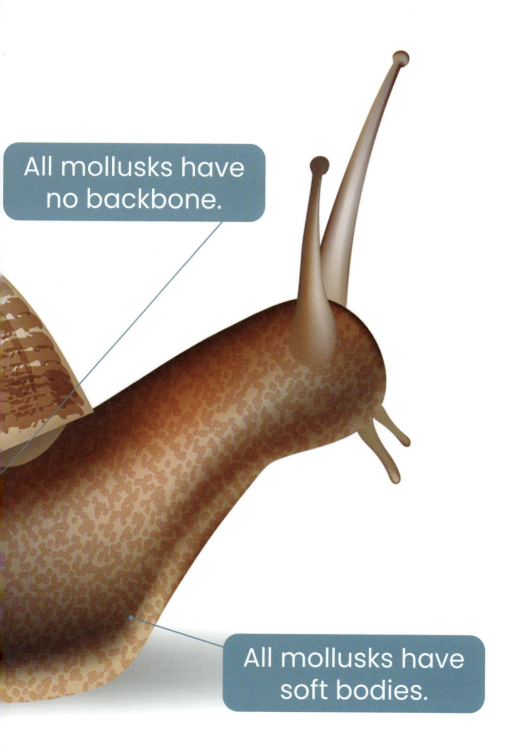

All mollusks have no backbone.

All mollusks have soft bodies.

Glossary

cuttlefish

scallops

octopuses

snail

Index

B
bodies, 5

C
clams, 8, 20

F
foot, 18, 20

S
slugs, 6